MW00452800

Follow us on Facebook+Twitter @GMNOTEBOOK

Invention convention

This

64674533R00073

Made in the USA
Middletown, DE
15 February 2018